GORILLA

poems by

Lee Stockdale

Joseph Geskey

Main Street Rag Publishing Company
Charlotte, North Carolina

Cover photo: John F. Kennedy and Grant Stockdale, the author's father, courtesy of the Harcourt-Harris Inc. Beulah Harris Ignall Photograph Collection, John F. Kennedy Presidential Library and Museum, Boston, MA
Author photo by Vera Miljković, Vera Miljković Studio, New York, NY

Acknowledgments:

I'm grateful to the journals that first published these following poems, sometimes in slightly different forms.

Reed Magazine, Bone Ink Chapbook: "Unforeseen Consequences of Cremation"
The Ekphrastic Review: "Ghost Through Torn Flag"
BlazeVOX: "George Washington at *Walmart*"
Kakalak: "The House Between the Towns"
Poetry That Sustains Us: "Angels in Colorado," "Let It Be Sunday"
2022 Pinesong Awards Anthology: "Getting to the Bottom of It"

Library of Congress Control Number: 2022942645

ISBN: 978-1-59948-938-4

Produced in the United States of America

Main Street Rag
PO Box 690100
Charlotte, NC 28227
www.MainStreetRag.com

For Gail
Of course

Contents

I. Limousines

Funland Park

My father and I walked beneath the sign,
I don't recall a special occasion,
or other siblings coming along.
Just the two of us in a part of Miami
slightly run down, which magnified the thrill.

He said, *Go on any ride you want.*

Kids' screams magnetized me to the bumper cars.
I climbed into one and stepped on the pedal,
easy to accelerate and fun to steer,
rounded the periphery to build speed
and gave a pony-tailed girl a *thunk*.
Boys and I bumped each other harder,
my father smiled, so this was okay,
preparing me for the ride to come.

She bumped me, I bumped back,
more softly this time. The electricity
shut off. The ride was over.
She and I sat in our motionless cars,
then exchanged a look when we saw new sparks
crackle from stems connected to the electrified ceiling.

My father stood there,
strong and knowledgeable,
in his Ban-Lon shirt.

Limousines

Kennedy is elected President!
There's so much happiness in the house,
and now he's coming to spend the night.

His limousine and a line of black cars
block the street beneath palm trees
and a clear November sky.
Men in dark suits wander the yard as Mr. Kennedy
and my father talk on the screened porch.

I sit on the floor and peel an orange,
I want to make him feel at home.

My mother asks what he'd like to drink.
A Coke, he says.
We have no *Cokes.*
My big sister drives to the A&P and brings home a case.
He wanted just one. Anyway now he's taking a nap,
so I have to be quiet and can't play outside.

They're all dressed up, going out for dinner,
my mother in the brown chiffon dress Dad loves.
I'll be in bed by the time they get back, see my opening,
step up and ask, *What can I do to be President?*

Learn your history, he says. *And mind your mother.*
My mother smiles,
before the President's brains are splattered
into the back of a limousine.
One week later my father commits suicide.

Anyone

The oversized photograph
and movie reel,
live in our home
in a rusted filing cabinet.

The photograph looks down
on a body,
on the roof of Miami's *DuPont Building*.

A thick, white, broken line,
traces the path from a window
on the thirteenth floor.
An arrow—the kind you peel off
and stick on,
is next to and points at the body,
face down, arms
at its sides, white dress shirt
untucked at the back.

Five men stand around the body.
Some smoke.

The movie,
from the same vantage point,
lasts three minutes: a white stretcher
pushed across from the right.
A priest climbs out a window,
kneels on one knee.

Smell of New Lumber

Lee Harvey Oswald
murders JFK.
My name also Lee,
does not help me not think
I am in some way responsible
for my father's death.
Should have been at the window

No! Dad!

Stop!

Wind in gray air wings,
flapping
to get back to the ledge.
Was he thinking,
on the way down, *This*

was a monumental
mistake, about the smell
of new lumber,
our unfinished treehouse,
going into that lumber yard,
picking out boards,
driving them home
sticking out the car window.

Was he thinking, *He'll finish it*
by himself. How hard
can it be to hammer nails
through wood.

Gorilla

I scale the Empire State Building to rescue the girl
who will become my wife,
but doesn't know it.
She ignores that I'm a hairy gorilla,
with pecs as big as the Yankee infield.

Because I am famished from scaling the building,
I'm afraid I will eat her whole,
like an anchovy.
Since I don't bring silverware when I scale.
It's all I can do to grab onto
the gargoyles and swing.
Sometimes I stick my big eye
in an office window.

But I don't eat her.
Instead, she and I walk to Central Park,
where we sit on a bench and I carve
"Gorilla + Future Wife" in a heart.

She says it if wasn't for Robert F. Kennedy in New York,
they'd still be treating the mentally ill like animals,
padlocked in cells with no air and no light,
kept barely alive with food shoved through slots
in the door by uniformed guards.
Never, or rarely, allowed to see family.
I'm going to learn so much from her.

Out Take

I was excited, as a sixth-grade boy, to ride
in the same car as the President and Mrs. Kennedy,
in the back seat of a limousine so big,
we had plenty of room to turn and look around
at the crowds of people who smiled and waved.
The President and Mrs. Kennedy waved
and smiled back and I thought, *Being the President*
must be fun.

At the end of the parade we had to slow down,
Dealey Plaza had lots of turns,
giving everybody a good chance to see
the President and Mrs. Kennedy up close.

Passing *The Texas School Book Depository*,
I thought it must be filled with *millions* of books,
since Texas was the largest state.

On our right, in a sunny, grassy area,
a man stood on a wall with a movie camera.
He didn't seem like an official person, but a dad
who'd love showing it to his family at home.

It felt like we'd driven through the whole city of Dallas,
before the car went faster because the President
had to get to the next place.
It would not be polite to start lunch without him!
I listened to his speech for a minute or two,
but got bored and went back to eat with the cooks.
They said, *You're a lucky boy.*

I Land

in the eye of a Zapruder hurricane:
Beatles, Stones, Dylan, Hendrix, Jefferson Airplane,
The Dead, Laura Nyro, *8 ½* , Hemingway,
Salinger, *Godot*, Joyce, *Candy*, Warhol, *Howl*,
Patti Smith, *Ginger Man*, Steinbeck, *Catch-22,*
Cuckoo's Nest, Night of the Iguana, CBGB, *Cafe Wha?*
Atticus Finch, Jackie-O, MLK, RFK,
Watergate, *Washington Post*, Aunt Lou/Teddy Ballgame,
Nam, Kent State, SDS, draft numbers, Black Panthers,
For the Roses, Court and Spark, In His Own Write,
It's a little bit funny, I'm OK, You're OK, Astral Weeks,
a well-respected man about town,
Orange Owsley—*Let the sunshine in,*
Thank You (Falettinme Be Mice Elf Again),
A Love Supreme, Tall and tan and young and lovely,
Hi-Fi Stereo—scratched—same skip,
there's a fog upon L.A., The Troubadour, Dan Hicks
and His Hot Licks, Al Jarreau, the *Baked Potato*
Nowhere Man, Don't Look Back, What's Going On?

Two Dreams

I write down my dreams when I wake up,
the sooner the better or I forget,
when I realized, *Oh, two dreams:*
First dream, where I'm doing nothing but dreaming,
Second dream, the dream *First dream* is dreaming.

For *First dream* I have nothing to write,
since all I'm doing is dreaming of dreaming.
In *Second dream* there's a party in the street,
people dance and drink in a holiday atmosphere.
I try to work my way into the fun by flapping
my arms and flying so they'll see me.
The main party person says, *Ignore him, he is not*
in this dream.

I don't think I'm supposed to be in either dream;
or my father was supposed to be in his dreams,
either.

I have to go back and tell *First dream:*
There's a party going on.
They're supposed to be my new friends
but think I'm a dream.

First dream is apathetic: *There's no party.*
You're dreaming.

I stop flying in *Second dream*
and instead merely walk the street,
unseen by strangers dancing and singing.

Machete

My mother's voice frantic at three a.m.,
wakes me as she phones police.
Within minutes, guns drawn, they're inside the house,
stabbing flashlights into darkened rooms,
a month to the day after my father's suicide.

Annie, my big sister, had been startled awake,
by shutters clicking in her downstairs bedroom.
She flicked a light on to see a man's hand
coming through the window.

The man had already been in the house,
pried open a window, popped out a screen,
propped it neatly against a wall,
lined up five knives on the kitchen counter,
of our family that, coincidentally, had five kids.

Annie's bedroom door had been locked.
He'd gone back outside around to her window.

Nothing was stolen, police are leaving,
satisfied whoever broke in is no longer there.
I point to the machete on the dining room table.
The officer asks my mother, *It's not yours?*
No, she says, *I've never seen it before.*
The police agree we can keep the machete.

The telephone rings.
Mother answers.
All of us hear the man's flat voice:
    I hear you've had some trouble tonight.
She thinks it's an official, following up,
Yes, the police just left.

The man repeats, less flat, more dark:
    I hear you've had some trouble tonight.
She's alert now, *Who is this?*
    We're going to get your daughter.
He hangs up.

Monk

Mr. Thompson, my art teacher, showed me
how to carve the monk
from a piece of firewood I brought from home,
now in New York after mother remarried.

The monk's main feature was the cross he wore,
a way to tell myself, *All this will pass*. Though
at thirteen those weren't conscious thoughts.

Mr. Thompson entered it in the middle school art show.
Out of the blue it won a blue ribbon.
I gave it to my older brother, Grant,
who went off to work one summer between college
at a Washington State *Birds Eye* pea canning factory.

Mother shipped the monk to Grant from New York,
in a steamer trunk by Greyhound bus,
with the Samurai sword and Japanese rifle
our father brought back from World War II,
among other heirlooms that belonged to our father.

She provided my brother with no information
about where, when, or how he should claim the trunk.
No word about why she was shipping it,
or how—when summer was over and he drove back East,
he'd fit the trunk in his VW bug.

The monk and our father's heirlooms were lost.
Grant later told me he'd found a disturbing message
in our mother's willful lack of care.
We knew, of course, there was more going on with her.

I think of the monk, out there somewhere,
in someone's den watching over the house.
Those years would pass, as the monk had assured.

Ghost Through Torn Flag

Each night Dufy's *Street Decked with Flags*
goes crooked on the wall in our house.
Mother copied the painting with watercolors,
I inherited two of her *Street Decked with Flags*;
she must have been going through her French period.
The main flag hangs in the center of the painting
from a rope stretched tight between two buildings.
People stroll beneath the flags: men in straw hats,
a woman in a white apron outside a restaurant, a woman
with an umbrella. In my mother's copies, but not Dufy's
original, the flag at bottom left is torn open.
Through this tear my mother made, a figure appears
—darkened, smudged, unlike the others,
whose ghost makes the painting go crooked each night.

Cut

At eighteen, I had just spent a week being Jesus,
in the psychiatric ward of a Connecticut hospital,
when my brother, Grant, graciously accepted
my improbable idea to come crash his life.

We woke in his apartment in Coconut Grove,
pushed his gray Volvo to get it started,
worked all day varnishing Russ Firestone's boat,
across the cut from Nixon's Key Biscayne White House.

Something in our conversation coming home
made him pull into the parking lot of the Coral Reef Yacht Club.
We belonged to the club when Dad was alive.
Dad had money. We belonged everywhere.

I'd followed Grant to the same military school,
we left with the pile of same gray shirts.
He'd cut off his collars—Miami Nehru,
I focused my eyes on loose threads around his neck.

I knew what he was saying, Dad destroyed himself.
We, his sons, sailed in his wake.
No one, but Grant, could have cut through, that day,
loneliness I thought was mine alone.

The Gift

A church asked me to give a reading
for *Suicide Prevention Month.*
I'd also bring my mother's book,
To Ireland With Love.
I inherited copies when she died,
and purchase others when they come up on *eBay.*

At random I pulled out the book she'd inscribed,
For Ted,
whom she'd met only days before,
and whom she'd marry a few weeks after that.

Arriving early, I arranged the room,
and began to leaf through my mother's book.
Fifty years later, I feel, anew,
the suicide wound in my mother's side.

The dust jacket includes a family photograph,
the seven of us posed in Phoenix Park,
on the grass in the sun,
outside the Ambassador's residence.
In this copy she'd gifted *For Ted,*
she had surgically scissored the family out.

Burning Flesh for Bing Crosby

Matches ignite and fuse to my hand.
I'd been placing packs next to loose cigarettes,
to help get ready for the big surprise gala.
I'm a distraction for mother who tells me,
Go into town for burn ointment with Bill.

Bill and I set out in the Ambassador's limousine,
unaware Dad wants it for Bing Crosby's arrival,
where the American singing star will be swarmed
at the airport by fans and reporters.

The chemist is closed. Bill knows of another.
He drives around Dublin until we conclude,
all chemists must close on Saturdays at noon.

Dad is fuming when we get home.
He thinks we've been joyriding,
while he met Mr. Crosby in the Ford station wagon.

I'm a model of contrition at dinner,
eventually able to sneak away to the ballroom,
filled with musicians and female dancers in kilts,
their ribbons scolding back mounds of hair.

Returning to the dining room, I see Mr. Crosby,
coming out of the men's room.
Where'd you run off to?
I made one mistake with him already today,
and cannot ruin his big surprise: *I was upstairs*
watching 'The Untouchables' on TV.

Dinner ends, doors open wide, musicians play,
and everyone is happy about the big surprise gala.

Next day I go with Mr. Crosby and Dad,
in the good car, where they'll play golf to raise money
for *The Society for the Prevention of Cruelty to Children.*
On the way there, with a box of golf balls in hand,
Mr. Crosby cracks me hard on the head.
Untouchables! he says.
He knew I'd lied.

Rifle

My father purchased the rifle
at the start of the trip
to *Bass Galore Village*
with Grant Jr. and me.

We drove clear across Florida
on the Tamiami Trail,
through Seminole country,
and saw young boys
with bows and arrows,
and no interest in us
as we passed in the car.

Sitting in the boat
in the middle of a lake,
we caught nothing but water bugs
skittering circles. And laughed
when Dad called it *No Bass*
Galore Village, where I shot
tin cans with a .22.

My father stopped the car
turning homeward,
and, inexplicably, threw the gun
in the river. That rifle

I have so often recalled,
has been here in my hands all along,
loaded.

Slab

I'm eleven.
On my head is a two-foot-thick slab,
like a steel vault door that stretches to infinity
in every direction.
I know I will kill myself.

Everyone said I was just like my father,
which made me proud.
I am just like my father, so I am
predestined, a fact,
like the sun or the moon.
I won't commit suicide
until I'm forty-seven,
like my father.

My big sister counseled me
to drop out of college
and get into therapy.
I'm about twenty-two when, one day,
walking down a sidewalk
near Dupont Circle in DC,
I see the sky plainly.
The slab is gone.

The Gorilla as a Boy

I was lucky she took me by the hand,
and pulled me from the shock of the freezing river,
where jagged ice moved past me at eye level,
legs too numb to kick, I couldn't breathe,
an electric eel coiled around my chest.

The river stripped off whatever I was.
I rolled to the side to hide from her sight.
She lifted my body to the Miami sun
no *Coppertone* lotion armored me from,
pumped my chest so I squirted a fountain
of water between blue lips.

She took me to *Boy's Town*,
bought me new pants, shirt, socks, shoes.
Now, she said, *you look like other boys.*
I stood in the mirror and had to admit,
I did look like a boy, not a gorilla.

From then on, everything seemed like a joke,
whatever a teacher said. Or my mother.
The funny thing was, nothing was funny.

Well, she asked, *have you had enough?*
She took me back to the icy river.
I turned it into the warm Mississippi,
where my father grew up on the banks, in Greenville.
I stood on the raft, a pirate, or boy,
just Huck Finn and me in the wide-open world.

II. Work, Work, Work, Work

Conversation with Mick Jagger

Night shift Manhattan has me hustling
from clubs to restaurants, theaters to apartments,
brownstones to bars, bars to hotels.

This is a cabdriver's secret joy:
to be up top of a long avenue,
and watch the red lights—a string of lit rubies,
turn green, like dominoes, all the way downtown.

I drop my fare off at the *Pierre Hotel*,
but can't get directly in front of the doorman.
A limo is idling, blocking the way,
waiting for the couple coming out of the lobby.

Bianca gets in on the sidewalk side,
Mick walks around on the night-black street.
Mick, who blasted my childhood open,
who I've danced and sung with on countless nights,
gotten high with girlfriends as we've laughed and played.
Mick now at the top of his rock and roll game: *Sticky Fingers, Exile on Main Street.*

The chauffeur opens the street-side door,
I leap from my cab and yell at Mick, *Goddammit!*
He asks the chauffeur, *What did he say?*
The chauffeur shakes his head,
Mick gets into the car,
they ease into the night.

Are You Jackie Kennedy?

I pick up my cab near the West Side docks,
shoot into midtown by my regular route,
when three men flag me down for 70th and Park.
I drop them off and on the opposite corner,
a woman I recognize raises her hand.

She gives me an address on Central Park West.
I know who it is but ask, *Are you Jackie Kennedy?*
    Yes, she says.
Do you know who I am!
    No.
I'm Grant Stockdale's son!
    How weird, she says and, leaning forward,
    You look just like your father.

Your voice, I tell her, *is so soft, it's hard*
to hear you through this bullet-proof glass.
    Yes, she says—pointing to the round holes
    we must talk through—*they even look like*
    bullet holes.

I'm suddenly embarrassed to be driving a cab,
the son of President Kennedy's Ambassador to Ireland.
I don't tell her I live next door to the Hell's Angels,
and chase rock and roll poetry up East Village fire escapes.

I'm taking time off from college. I don't really know
what I want to be. Maybe a psychiatrist. Or an Episcopal priest.
    Oh, John and Caroline don't know
    what they want to do either.
And just like that, she makes me feel like one of her kids.

Light chatter now—the city, February cold.
She comes around, pays the fare at my window.
    If there's anything I can do for you, just let me know.
She begins walking away, then turns back to give me
the famous Jackie Kennedy smile.

That's The Way God Planned It

Love was etched on every bullet I fired,
a woman of influence said my service disturbed her.
I served in the way I felt God required.

From time immemorial, evil conspired
with greed for power, genocide, murder.
Love was etched on every bullet I fired.

She implied my morals were haywire.
My devotion to duty should not have unnerved her,
I served in the way I felt God required.

Ideals of freedom were, to my mind, higher,
than whatever she held in her mind to gird her.
Yet love was etched on every bullet I fired—

love of God and country kept me inspired.
She won't be turned, I don't try to convert her,
I served in the way I felt God required.

From Private to Colonel and I retired,
I'm sorry if my service hurt her.
Love was etched on every bullet I fired.
I served in the way I felt God required.

The House Between the Towns

We'll stop at dusk at the house I pass
between Kaiserslautern and Mühlbach
as the First Sergeant's driver,
with its colored lights strung from posts like a café.

They will be like family.
They will be more like family
than our own families.
I know you sense this, too.

We will sit and laugh at the tables
set up outside and very close to the road,
as the Felliniesque father—why do we think he's a dentist,
or was once a dentist—tells stories and clowns.

It's comforting, and unusual, to have someone at the center
so gracious with the hospitality of his personality,
to say nothing of the wine and French bread that don't stop.

Young people on scooters come and go all night.
Their laughter, hair, and radical ideas
fly in the breeze.

How many times have I passed this house
and known what I know now?

We will never return to our old lives.
We'll be like migrating birds
who don't go home.
We'll find things to do,
make ourselves useful,
ride scooters.

Curiosity

I'm assigned *Temporary Duty*
as a JAG officer,
to train Afghan Army Lawyers,
when, at a Kabul street corner,
the eyes of a Taliban man
stare into mine in the van,
and tell me, *I must kill you.*

I sense his inward curiosity
about why he must kill me.

I sense my own
about why I would kill him.

But when the light changes,
the driver speeds around the corner
on two wheels.

UNITED STATES OFFICE OF PERSONNEL MANAGEMENT(SENSITIVE INFORMATION REDACTED)

WASHINGTON, DC 20415

Dear :

As you may know, the Office of Personnel Management (OPM) was the target
of a malicious cyber intrusion carried out against the U.S. Government
which resulted in the theft of

You are receiving this notification because we have determined that you
was included I share
your concern and frustration and want you to know we are working hard to
provide you at no cost

immediate family personal acquaintances

a spouse and in some cases, citizens

While we are not aware of you we are providing a comprehensive suite
of theft services. We offer you children under the age of 18
as of July 1, 2019, that specialize in theft The theft
has already begun.

You have access to these services at any time during the next three years.

I hope you will not contact any person anyone

person relation do not
For additional resources such as people protect your
person

Sincerely,

Acting Director
Office of Personnel Management

---

www.opm.gov *Recruit, Retain and Honor a World-Class America*

Miesau Backhome Gospel Choir

My ears reverberate
with call and response,
tambourines and handclaps
ricochet off walls,
our red satin robes swish, flash, light fires,
in front of the altar
where choirs compete.

Choir that affords me relief from the towers,
guarding America's nuclear weapons,
for endless hours around the clock,
staring down into *Deadly Force Authorized*,
that space of grass
between the razor wire and woods,
alternately reading *Humboldt's Gift*
and imagining a future back in the world.

People dance in the aisles,
shoot hands in the air,
a woman slain in the spirit
falls to the floor,
I'm happy for her sake is carpeted.

The organ player builds a—*what?*
a ramp, a staircase,
that spirals to heaven,
where anyone
can get up there
and meet God face-to-face.

The Singing Sons of Zweibrücken win again.
What do you expect? They've been together ten years.
We walk out into the night's light rain,
and board the bus for the long ride home.

Understanding

My client, up for armed robbery,
dispenses facts like gifts.
I'm his public defender,
and hold my laptop up to the glass
of the jail's claustrophobic interview room,
to play him the video
the DA just gave me.

He watches intently.
He's searching his mind.
Then decides forcefully, *That's not me!*
I've been photoshopped in. Those aren't my hands.
He holds up his hands.
What about your face and head looking around?
They got it from Facebook, the Internet,
I don't know, from anywhere.

He tells me to interrogate everybody
who handled the video, *You'll find who it was*
made it look like me.

I remind him of his almost identical charge:
the bodega robbery two years ago.
He's still on parole, the reason bail was denied.
I made a mistake, but that's not me this time.
I swear to God, I've been photoshopped in.

We talk for a while, I gather his file,
and rise to leave, when he looks up:
I'll plead guilty. Get me the best deal you can.

Revolvers

The revolving door spins hotel guests
like chambered rounds in a cylinder,
aimed through swans etched in frosted glass,
where people circle around all day,
across from my shoeshine stand,
where I polish leather for women and men
who carry briefcases and accoutrements for battle,
and advance toward appointments and social engagements.
A linked-arm couple revolves as one,
a tricky and potentially dangerous maneuver.
A woman in dark glasses squeezes a poodle,
and shields its eyes when they hit the sun.
It's not enough that I shine their shoes,
I pray for each revolver,
that they don't get jammed in the heavy brass door,
but make it safely onto the street.
Some are only short prayers,
they revolve so quickly.

Dante's Eye Bags

This morning I looked in the mirror to discover
I have significant eye bags that snuck in
over the years and gradually set up shop,
until they are now mature and grand enough
to announce: *Hello! We're here! We are your eye bags!*

I want to hate them, except—
they make me look like Dante Fascell,
the Congressman from Miami who beat my father
in the democratic primary in 1954,
then held that seat for forty years.

In 1990, at a Homestead, Florida, 4th of July Parade,
Dante and I sat together in the VIP bleachers,
he as a Congressman, I as Homestead's
National Guard Commander.
I introduced myself as my father's son,
and Dante apologetically tried to explain
the confusing politics that induced him at the last minute,
to enter the race and beat my father who,
before Dante jumped in, ran unopposed.

I stopped listening, more interested in Dante's
deeply jowled face, the eye bags
that drooped like rippled sacks of flour
from his lower eyelids onto his cheeks.
So this morning, no, I do not hate my eye bags,
they make me feel like I could beat my father
in a democratic primary for Congressman from Miami.

Criminal Justice

Lawyers strip money
from clients in vestibules
the DA wheels by
with an evidence crate
crammed with running shoes kitchen knife
leather purse pearl choker
jurors rehearse *Guilty Not guilty*
as the court reporter rains hands
on her tiny machine
witnesses remember disremember
can't recall
testimony implodes
they reach
for Kleenex
as sports-talk radio leaks
from an earpiece
of a bailiff stuffing prisoners
into the time-out box
and separate stale clouds
of last night's breath
hang above pews
packed with girlfriends boyfriends
wives ex-wives baby mamas
who try to catch eyes
of their luckless downcast.

Hear ye! Hear ye!
the judge leaps the rail
and flees the courthouse with inmates
following
bailiffs guards girlfriends
everyone runs now
ducking up side streets
jumping down manholes
dashing to escape from
criminal justice.

Stasi Woman

The Battalion Intelligence Officer says she's Stasi,
posted outside church in the American Sector,
assigned to monitor officer traffic,
as many high-ranking generals are Catholic,
such as *Otis My Man*, Commander-in-Chief, Europe,
who often has business in Berlin.

She looks about thirty, five-feet-four,
acts like she may be on the spectrum.
Sporadic eye contact,
never goes inside church,
her slit cap festooned with enamel pins.
Occasionally, she'll hold a spray of flowers,
against the black cape she invariably wears,
linked at the neck by a short, brass chain.

I pass her when I go to my Pre-Cana Class,
where I learn to be Catholic,
so I can marry my fiancée in Solomons, Maryland,
at *Our Lady Star of the Sea Catholic Church*.

My wife, when she joins me in Berlin,
wonders why the woman is there. I tell her
what the Intelligence Officer told me.

Then, one day, the woman is gone.
No one misses her or mentions her absence.
She must have gotten a new assignment.
A promotion, I hope. She did a good job.

Battlefield

Balm of silence,
the cannons have stopped,
chaff of DD 214s
float into my foxhole,
with the smell of rifle bore cleaner,
and the vision of a woman
handing me five yellow daisies.

This silence, how long?
One minute. Twelve hours.
Is it still a battlefield?
Has history ended?

I see fellow soldiers,
disinterested and tired,
rise and walk toward the horizon,
silhouetted against distant fires.

I should join them,
but I have my orders:
I will guard everything
within the limits of my post,
and not quit my post
until properly relieved.

Low gray clouds
slide above me like coffins.
A stranger approaches,
peers into my foxhole,
hands down a message:
    Your war is over.

III. Let It Be Sunday

Unforeseen Consequences of Cremation

I am floating at the top of Bob Johnson's evening martini,
a flake of me settles on splintered wood bleachers
of the Polk County little league baseball field,
some of me gets run over by the left rear tire
of a Winnebago heading for the Cherokee National Forest.
When I told my family I wanted to be cremated,
my ashes poured into the Chockalute River
where my father taught me to fish,
where I taught my three boys to fish,
it never occurred to me my ashes might end up
on the left rear tire of a Winnebago, as nothing
guarantees your windborne particles
won't be inhaled by a dog in the park,
or get caught in the hair of sunbathers
as they talk in a roundabout way of marriage.
He says he wants them,
she says she does not,
causing for the first time a realization
of fundamental differences between them,
so that, later, at Tryon's Sidestreet Pizza,
stealing glances at each other over pepperoni,
they must secretly wonder if their love
is strong enough to bridge the chasm
opening between them like the Grand Canyon,
to which part of me travels even now
on the left rear tire of a Winnebago.

Pastoral

I sit in the waiting area while they change my oil.
This Boulder *Jeep* dealer makes me feel rugged,
the waiting area is an *Adventure Outfitters.*
Kayaks and mountain bikes hang from rafters,
a woman in Spandex will plan my trip
up the side of a mountain or to shoot the rapids.
It doesn't have to be in a *Jeep.*

I smell the pines as I leave my tent,
stretch my arms to the sky: *I love nature!*
and kneel at the campfire for morning coffee,
gratis from the dealer's vending machine,
before I go flyfishing in the Colorado.

Denise B. from service wanders into my campsite,
gives me hard news about my brake pads.
I don't want worn brakes to fly me off a cliff,
though mostly I drive back and forth to work.
It'll take a few hours, I tell her I'll wait,
see if the fish are biting, try out my new rod.

Later she brings me friendly updates. We talk
about David Attenborough's new documentary:
climate change, the end of the world.
So depressing, she says, *it made me cry.*

But, I remind her, *he ends with hope*—that solar
and wind power replace fossil fuels, carbon-
belching cars will be a thing of the past.
Denise B. darkens, thinks this might kill her job.
I assure her, *We'll still need our oil changed.*
She's already walking back through the woods.

Gauntlet

They've been talking about this rain for days,
months if you count *The Farmer's Almanac*,
TV meteorologists, parents, people standing in lines.
Teachers prepare students with Noah's Ark information:
Up the ramp go Instagram, Spotify, Netflix, Tik Tok.
All the streaming services you'll need to survive
when the flood recedes. If it ever does.

Store shelves are bare as a baby's bottom,
no bread, *Diet Pepsi*, or wood to nail over windows,
no duct tape to cover and blind the eyes
from the disaster no one wants to see.
Everyone is dying to see.

Still, the rain is all people talk about,
moving their lips behind the masks.
Rain down, rain,
come stroke the head of the laughing beast.

Johnny Cash Concert

Johnny Cash rocks the Kingdome
with a concert more than worth the price of admission,
free at a Billy Graham Crusade.

I can't leave after he finishes playing,
be the solitary soul who exits the stadium.
I'm resigned to sit through Billy Graham,
and steel myself to the coming harangue.

He begins with an anecdote,
like any friendly next-door neighbor,
then builds up steam, punctuates words,
cuts his arm through the air.

His voice is a lance, catches me up,
punches into my chest—
Christ died for your sins.
I am a sinner, this I know from personal experience.
I don't want to go down in a ring of fire.

My defenses crumble, my mind does a one-eighty.
He invites us to come down onto the field
where the Seahawks will play the Dallas Cowboys.
My limbs activate, propelled by the spirit,
I descend the stairs to accept Christ,
as I watch my old life walk off and vanish.

Angels in Colorado

Driving back to Yellow Springs, Ohio,
in the middle of nowhere I need a rest stop.
Mark brakes the car.
We haven't seen a soul for hundreds of miles—
no one goes out in a blizzard.

Mark avails himself of the opportunity,
I go to the front, he to the rear,
no trees, oceans of snow.

The sky fills with angels,
a mosaic umbrella,
horizon to horizon,
seamless dome of dozens, not more.
I say this to give you an idea of their size.
Large angels I'd say, silver-colored,
strangely impassive.

Back in the car I'm silent, stunned,
I have to assume Mark saw them, too,
and that, equally moved, we say nothing at all.

The blizzard worsens, he gives me the wheel.
I edge through mountains
beside sheer drop-offs.
The road's an unfolding white-out guess.
I'm only sure of the whipping wind.

Let It Be Sunday

I help serve the communion wine
when the organist starts into *Let It Be*,
which is not her usual fare,
and I begin to feel surreal repeating,
The blood of Christ,
The cup of salvation,
as I move from one communicant to the next
when they come from their pews.

I try to adopt a solemn persona, except now
I'm reflecting on the Beatles' *White Album*,
less collaborative than *Abbey Road*,
produced when they were breaking up,
which was more cohesive than *Let It Be*, their last,
which I'm now comparing with The Last Supper,
telling his disciples, *Do this*
in remembrance of me. Remarkable
we're still doing it two-thousand years later.

The organist must be a Beatles fan,
cranking it louder toward the end.
I have to raise my voice to be heard,
The blood of Christ,
The cup of salvation,
caught up in the passion of Christ,
but also the passion of *Hey Jude, Sgt. Pepper*,
their earlier songs—*She Was Just Seventeen*,
until the last person comes to the rail.

People's People

I contacted him to arrange the event,
but his people were busy and told my people
to contact his people's people,
who asked when my people might be free.
I told his people my people were free,
as my people are me and I am always free.

His people asked, *What about publicity?*
I told them, *We've got that covered. My people*
Scotch-taped flyers to windows
of stores that would let us, in our small town.
But, his people asked, *what about NPR?*
Oh, yes, we can pull it in here. Driving home
we listen to 'All Things Considered.'
We like it best at the end of the hour
when they talk about music and artsy stuff.

We became phone friends, his people's people and I,
discussing red wines he likes, But no green M&Ms!
When he arrived, surrounded by his people,
his Say Hello & Shake Hands people
said *Hello* and shook hands.

The turnout for the event was disappointing.
It was mostly his people and his people's people.
All my people were there in force.

Socialist Shoes

The *Evergreen State* is ever green
because it rains almost every day.
I sat in the train beside a nun
who picked her teeth after every meal,
then smiled and apologized behind cupped hands.
She lit up when I told her I was going back to college.

I noticed, as soon as I got off the train,
that everything everywhere was Zen garden clean,
and everyone wore thick-rubber-soled shoes,
designed to walk through puddles of rain,
for women and men the identical style,
like you'd see in a socialist state,
where there's only one factory and that's what you get.
I had never seen shoes like these on the East Coast,
like miniature pieces of IKEA furniture,
fitted on ends of people's legs.

University women had soft Swedish complexions
—there's no sun.
I'd look down at their feet and, *Oh.*
Such gentle people—like Tolkien wood elves,
victims of a cruel fashion prank.

I graduated and went home to New York,
city of grime and normal shoes.
If I can walk through puddles there,
I can walk through puddles anywhere,
New York, New York.

George Washington at *Walmart*

Of course it's George Washington
in the dairy section
of the *Super Walmart* on Highway 61.

He looks out of place in his white stockings,
britches over his knees,
and powdered wig unless that's his real hair.

Out of place yet at the same time at home,
like he owns this *Walmart* and everything in it,
plastic lawn chairs from China, dish towels, chainsaws,
owns the entire United States of America,
Statue of Liberty, redwood forests,
every song ever written by Woody Guthrie.

He looks puzzled by choices—
non-fat, 2%, whole, enriched.
I want so much to help him decide,
want to show him a dairy farm,
electric pumps hooked up to cows,
want to google *America* on Wikipedia for him,
watch him be dumbfounded
by the country he fathered.
Except it's a well-observed unwritten rule:
No one talks to each other when they shop at a *Walmart*.

CONGRESS OF THE UNITED STATES
(SENSITIVE INFORMATION REDACTED)
WASHINGTON, DC 20510

October 7, 2021

The Honorable Joseph R. Biden, Jr., President
The White House
1600 Pennsylvania Avenue
Washington, D.C. 20500

Dear President Biden,

We urge you to release John F. Kennedy also known as JFK, unanimous maximum public release. The majority of Americans believe Kennedy, which seems the intent. Democracy requires minds

people trust government ideals society

history pain hope opportunity.

Act release Kennedy utmost and urgent.

Thank you for your consideration
Sincerely,

Anna G. Eshoo
Member of Congress

Steve Cohen
Member of Congress

James P. McGovern
Member of Congress

Jamie Raskin
Member of Congress

Sara Jacobs
Member of Congress

Joe Neguse
Member of Congress

cc: David of the United States

Magnificence of the Eternal Night Sky

My wife and I licked
the same stamp
on a paper airplane
that sailed out
into the universe.

Serendipity

Repeated butterflies chased by frogs with nets,
on the wallpaper sample at *Williamson's Paint Store*,
frogs never catching, never catching, never—,
butterflies unaware of the frogs or the danger.

Our son's music video of romantic loss: *Butterfly*,
he sent last night by *YouTube* link.

This morning orange Monarchs on a bush by the kitchen,
pulsing to a slow, rhythmic drum,
on a spirit frequency that is, once was, or is to come.

In yoga today, after we finish the hard parts,
before we're allowed to lie flat on our backs,
the teacher says, *Put the soles of your feet together,*
let your knees fall out for—some Sanskrit word,
then in English, *Butterfly pose.*

Late afternoon at the Landrum Library,
Leah searches for books she has to read before school starts.
I'm incredulous to find in the lobby,
framed, under glass, on a presentation table,
a collection of different-sized blue iridescents.
Excited, I tell her, *Leah! Look!*
Leah's not interested, she's looking for books.

An Accounting

The service station man
who pumped my mother's gas,
would snap the red rag
from his back pocket,
pop the hood,
check her oil,
pull out the dipstick,
wipe, reinsert,
check the level,
and show my mother
her oil was fine.

When he washed the windshield
on her side,
he'd look at her
through the glass and smile,
make small circles
with his paper towel,
as if he pretended
to polish her nose.
I'd glance over
to make sure she smiled back.
She always did,
though with tighter lips.

My mother never paid,
or signed a receipt,
and on reflection,
now that I know more,
she must have had a running account,
and paid by check,
when he sent her the bill.

EXXON RESEARCH AND ENGINEERING COMPANY

P.O. BOX 51. LINDEN, N.J. 07036

(PROPRIETARY INFORMATION REDACTED)

PRODUCTS RESEARCH DIVISION
Scientific Advisor

June 6, 1978
The Greenhouse Effect
Ref. No: 78PR 461

THE GREENHOUSE EFFECT

Products Research Division
Exxon Research and Engineering Co.

The Greenhouse Effect refers to   the
earth   the sun   some Swedish
aircraft flights   American Samoa   and the
South Pole. Atmospheric scientists generally
attribute this to 75 billion metric tons of
carbon dioxide   by Exxon.

Scientists agree that   carbon dioxide
has   been eliminated.   In fact, a
look at billions of metric tons of carbon
per year   represents   a considerable
amount of sensational publicity.

Now, you will remember that   the
atmosphere is due to   First,
favors.   However, most scientists
feel that more research is needed to support
the destruction of forests and other land.
The effect of a cloud will depend upon the
earth entering a period of serious question.

Occasionally, a model is found to converge
initially upon a definite answer but after a

short period of time to jump off this solution and settle down upon another one. After a second indefinite period, it will jump up and converge again upon a third solution and so on producing a number of apparent solutions in a random manner. Lorenz pointed out that the climate will settle down but then after a random period will jump every 10 to 15 minutes. Manabe and Wetherald estimate an expected natural cooling trend. There will probably be a rise of 70 meters in the world's oceans. On a global basis, this should result in a lengthening of the growing season.

conclusions

man is premature should not be encouraged. Detailed recommendations prepared by an Advisory Committee.

High resolution radar and aerial photography will probably be required in some instances to identify mankind burning.

The Donkey Speaks

How do I get picked for these tasks?
I can barely keep my eyes on the road,
with all these joyful fools crowding in.

Hosannas and *Halleluiahs* stab sheaves of wheat
in my ears. No one should wonder why
I slide them back.

This fellow I carry, it's like he's a king,
a one-man circus.
Big celebration. Where's the party?

Nobody briefed me, information zero.
They're laying palm fronds in my path,
and now, literally, the shirts off their backs.

Later, at the donkey barn, there's naturally talk
about all the hoopla: *Aren't you the lucky one.*
I got extra hay.

Now I'm a celebrity, star of the barn,
telling them how great it was, with all the
palm fronds and *Halleluiahs*.

A few days later we hear the news.
Wasn't that him who rode in on your back?
No, I say, *I never knew him*.

King of the Delta Blues

It's the last fair deal gone down
Last fair deal gone down
It's the last fair deal gone down, good Lord
On the Gulfport Island Road
-Robert Johnson

How did Robert know to be at the crossroads?
Which way did the signposts point when he got there?
The deal with the devil—did he have a choice?
What was he offered?
For what in exchange?

Robert left town an average juke joint player,
returned as the world's greatest blues musician,
nuclear epicenter of ElvisBeatlesStonesDylan.
He played street corners,
in front of barber shops,
for money white people tossed at his feet.
Turned his head, shy, the two times he recorded.

Night was when Robert let loose his blues,
when no white people could bar his way.
Women loved him.
Men loved his talent.
Not the jealous man who poisoned him.
No devil around to save him then.
Robert's last fair deal gone down.

Explicable

Driving east on Cane Creek,
that unusual straightaway,
with foothills on either side drifting up,
I have never beheld more vivid colors
than those painted onto
the Blue Ridge Mountains.
As if something is filtering light
from the sun,
giving everything
an Old Master feel.

Until it occurs to me,
this is my first day back
among the living,
after Covid-19
had taken me down,
when I felt
like a group of invisible men
was beating my chest
with bowling pins,
and what tiny pockets of air
I could breathe,
were buckets lowered down
to a barricaded cave.

Day by slow day, the Covid
subsided, until this morning
the telephone nurse
released me from quarantine.
Driving east on Cane Creek,
what I must be seeing,
is health and strength
flowing back to me.

Cleaning Out the Old Woman's Garage

I was too young to have a paper route,
so the woman who lived alone on our block,
—her husband died before I was born,
paid me to clean out her garage:
broken chairs, bed frames, shovels, hoes,
wooden golf clubs, rolled-up carpet

that smelled. I knocked at her back door.
She was studying over papers at the kitchen table.
I held up a rope that hung on the wall,
Can I use this to tie stuff together?

My husband worked it in a hurricane to lash himself
to a palm. I've got no use for it. That's a good use.

I stood speechless
and looked down at the rope.

She took off her glasses, *Oh, no doubt about it.*
Without that rope or he'd've been killed.
Tied himself to a palm tree in the Keys—
Islamorada—Upper Keys.
The 1935 Labor Day Hurricane.
Hundreds were killed, veterans in work camps,
building the Florida East Coast Railway.

Ode to the Roof

Handsome shingles I took you for granted,
aged by the sun from dark green to white,
in twenty-five years you never once leaked,
never complained when we screwed into your head
a succession of soon-obsolete satellite dishes.

Every expert delivers the same prognosis:
We're sorry to tell you, your roof must be put down.

You caught dozens (maybe hundreds?) of blue and orange
Frisbees; sheltered babies, teenagers, prom dates
with orchids. On your back you carried tons of snow
that might have crushed our family to death.

I do not blame your loosened granules
that clogged the gutters after it rained,
so that water pooled around the house
and caused foundation and moisture problems.
Weathered Warrior, I cannot expect you
to understand money, do not feel guilty,
but the costs of repair went through the roof.

The day you were born, the workers rejoiced,
Congratulations! Your new thirty-year roof.
And yet, you just turned twenty-five.
If human, your prime.

Can you not stay with us five more years?
A new roof is not in the budget.
The roofers say, sadly, we must pull the plug.
None among them sadder than I.

Debbie Reynolds

What's my name, Pop?
Do you know who I am?
Do you recognize Jody?
Jody's your granddaughter.
Say 'Hi' to Jody, Pop.
What color was our first dog?
What color was the Buick?
What year did you get married?
What was Mom's maiden name?
What did you do for a living?
Where did we live?
Did it snow very much?
Who shoveled the snow?
Who lived next door?
You liked movies, what was your favorite?
What actress did you like best?
Come on, Pop, think,
from 'The Unsinkable Molly Brown.'
You loved the way she danced.
Remember? She was short.
...
No, not a child, or, yes,
not much taller, but an adult,
an adult lady actress.
Think, Pop, think back,
you loved her like crazy.
What was her name?
It starts with a D.

Movie Theater

The ship sails into the sunset,
a skull and bones flaps in the wind,
the kidnapped boy looks back at the island
as the head pirate laughs and startles the parrot.

Tight shot on the green bottle that bobs in the waves,
then washes up on the island beach.
The boy awakes to his mother's voice,
Timmy! Get up. Time for breakfast.
Behold, the bottle, there on his nightstand.
He reads the message inside,
smiles—
The End.

The meager audience never sees the message.
An ungratifying ending, they exit grumbling
for these thin plot movies the owner runs,
in a theater that should have closed years ago,
kept afloat only by unknowing snowbirds.

He closes the theater and goes home to his attic
room with sloping ceilings and mouse batting
string in a corner.
Speak, little mouse, what's on your mind?
Do you want to be me and wear sandals and shorts?
The man wants to be an acorn, fall from a tree,
grow green hair, be a slow growth movie.
He can hear them now, *Give me back my money.*
He always does, he's commercially minded.
One will die today, don't let his last thought be,
That man who would not give me my money back.

Let his last thoughts be of the wife he loved,
the condo they enjoyed in Central Florida,
how lucky he was to be born an American,
how lucky to die on such a fine day.

Getting to the Bottom of It

One of the obstacles at Fort Benning's Officer
Candidate School was a long, narrow plank,
above a lake, between two telephone poles.
In the middle of the plank, was a step, two high,
I successfully crossed over by repeating in my mind:
Thank you, Jesus. Thank you, Jesus.

The family loves hiking to Bradley Falls,
where every two years someone falls and is killed,
disregarding the *STAY BACK!* signs.
I stay more well back than anyone in the family.

We went on vacation to New York City,
and stayed on the hotel's seventh floor.
The two times I stood at the open window,
I felt an unseen hand
try to flip me out the window,
down into the street below.

The next time I made a hotel reservation,
this time for a conference in Newark, New Jersey,
I told the receptionist, *My father jumped out a window
and killed himself. Can you please give me a room
on the first or second floor?*
I had never made this request before,
and was grateful for her understanding, and mine.

Crypto Poetry

is like the old kind, words are still "written" down like before, except they're no longer "words," but blockchain bits on Merkle trees, so whatever "words" a poet "timestamps" (writes) is "viewed" (read) virtually through its certificate of authenticity.

Someone who views the original timestamp, does not actually view the original Merkle bits, but an auto-generated computer near representation, which sounds inoptimal, but it's not: Crypto poetry is a thousand times better, *It's been synthesized through countless computers.* "Countless" is, of course, hyperbolic: by the time a crypto block gets to a viewer—all of whom must be certified authentic—the certificate of authenticity comes with the precise number of computers through which the blockchain bits have traveled. So the owner, by logging onto cryptopoetrycentralsystem dot com, may watch in real time as the number snowballs and explodes exponentially.

Like the "poem" my friend, Alex, sent me from Santa Fe, strained through crypto farms in Iceland, Russia, China, the Ukraine, and—wait! new numbers are coming in now! yes, from a location in Langley, Firginia, which gives me a warm feeling that it's the real thing, and I'm viewing Alex's authentic blockchain bits, and if any problem ("error") is found—an unusual image, say, or concept "not recognized"—cryptobots homogenize in a split-second so nano it's faster than anything recorded on earth or in space.

My Friend Accepts the Difficult Truth About Nixon

Mold grew on my friend's brain,
a phenomenon doctors had never encountered.
They flew him to Paris for the neuro conference,
his head in a bubble, fed soup through a tube.

Alone in the Louvre's I.M. Pei glass pyramid,
he asked himself, *Where did I go wrong?*
traced his life from his mother's womb,
through kindergarten, grade school, soccer team, Harvard.
A torrent of images burst the dam: *Nixon, Watergate,*
Archibald Cox, a seersuckered John Dean,
the televised hearings.   He tried

to close his mind to the onslaught,
as he never, *never* believed his president,
Richard Nixon could be so stupid.
Nixon, who opened the door to China,
whom my friend had believed was an innocent
victim: blameless, intelligent, consummate
statesman. He meditated, in the pyramid, on Henry

Kissinger, old but still living, head
of an international consulting firm in New York:
    Come to me, Henry. Reveal the truth.
Henry's message was hard to swallow: *It's true,*
Nixon was surrounded by dishonest boobs.
But Nixon himself had no morals, either.

Accepting the truth, my friend's mold disappeared.
He banged on the pyramid, *Let me out.*
He walked along the Seine,
visited the bookstore that published *Ulysses*,
laid a wreath on Jim Morrison's grave,
and returned to America, healed, and refreshed.

Poetry Reading

Welcome and it's wonderful to have you here at *Books & Etc.* this evening,
for this very special reading by Samuel Kushner-Alvrides,
recipient of the prestigious Treester Award,
as every jot and tittle of Sampson's work
is filled with tears of heaven
or river of hell,
as one need bring no insight
to an O'Cushman-Albright poem,
to appreciate the stark beauty of truth in the—
what can we call it?
Who can hang a name
on the door to the place where we ourselves live,
at once know
and *not* know
what's happening on the other side,
behind the sign that reads, *Gone fishin'*, or *Out of Order*.
No one better than Sean O'Malley himself,
curator of the thrift store of broken dreams
that swing on rusted coat hangers
against the back wall of the mind,
to read that sign from the very lips that wrote it.
So, ladies and gentlemen, without further ado,
please give a big *Books & Etc.* welcome to Sean T. O'Kelly-O'Devlin.

23rd Psalm, annotated

The Lord is my shepherd though I'm not a sheep. He maketh me to lie down in green pastures. He restoreth my soul, even if it's a gorilla's, and leads me beside still waters.

He leads me in the paths of righteousness, and I've been down paths not paved with righteousness, so I look forward to finding out where the new paths go.

Yea, though I walk through the valley of the shadow of death, I will fear no evil, for thou art with me. And wert with me when assassination and suicide rocked my life.

Thy rod and thy staff they comfort me, so if I were a sheep, thou'll make sure I don't stray and get roasted by bandits.

Thou preparest a table before me in the presence of mine enemies, perhaps the same bandits thou just outwitted.

Thou anointest my head with oil and I'm confident thou knowest how much I can take.

My cup runneth over, so things can get messy, the reason I keep this psalm by my side, knowing surely goodness and mercy shall follow me all the days of my life, and I will dwell in the house of the Lord forever.

Amen.

With thanks, especially, to

Phil White, Cathy Smith Bowers, Greg Lobas, Robert Polito, Morri Creech, Jon Pineda, Sally Keith, Fred Leebron/Queens University, Kathleen Graber, Tina Barr, Christian Haub, Vera Miljković, Chris Kamm, Robert Ard, Scott White, Stephen "Stevo My Bevo" Barber, Mike deGruy, John Heffernan, Mark Scriptunas, Mark Manivong/ Library of Congress Rare Books Division, St. Mark's in-the-Bowery Poetry Project, John F. Kennedy Library and Museum, CBGB, Vermont College of Fine Arts, Geraldine R. Dodge Poetry Festival, Tryon Fine Arts Center, sisters Ann and Susan Stockdale, children Leah, Benjamin, Noah, Sara, Zachary, and with greatest love to my wife Gail.